Our Splendid Failure to Do the Impossible

Our Splendid Failure to Do the Impossible

Rebecca Lindenberg

AMERICAN POETS CONTINUUM SERIES NO. 209
BOA EDITIONS, LTD. * ROCHESTER, NY * 2024

Copyright © 2024 by Rebecca Lindenberg
All rights reserved
Manufactured in the United States of America

First Edition
23 24 25 26 7 6 5 4 3 2 1

For information about permission to reuse any material from this book, please contact The Permissions Company at www.permissionscompany.com or e-mail permdude@gmail.com.

Publications by BOA Editions, Ltd.—a not-for-profit corporation under section 501 (c) (3) of the United States Internal Revenue Code—are made possible with funds from a variety of sources, including public funds from the Literature Program of the National Endowment for the Arts; the New York State Council on the Arts, a state agency; and the County of Monroe, NY. Private funding sources include the Max and Marian Farash Charitable Foundation; the Mary S. Mulligan Charitable Trust; the Rochester Area Community Foundation; the Ames-Amzalak Memorial Trust in memory of Henry Ames, Semon Amzalak, and Dan Amzalak; the LGBT Fund of Greater Rochester; and contributions from many individuals nationwide. See Colophon on page 123 for special individual acknowledgments.

Cover Art: "April Showers/May Flowers" by Appleton
          Instagram @ Appletonpictures
Cover Design: Daphne Morrissey
Interior Design and Composition: Isabella Madeira
BOA Logo: Mirko

BOA Editions books are available electronically through BookShare, an online distributor offering Large-Print, Braille, Multimedia Audio Book, and Dyslexic formats, as well as through e-readers that feature text to speech capabilities.

Cataloging-in-Publication Data is available from the Library of Congress.

BOA Editions, Ltd.
250 North Goodman Street, Suite 306
Rochester, NY 14607
www.boaeditions.org
A. Poulin, Jr., Founder (1938-1996)

"Poetry is nothing if not equipped for crisis. Sharp and penetrating, it cuts through every fear by which we are secretly governed, brings each to the light of the page and names it...The goal is to make not sense but art of this story. The goal is not to make a story but to experience the whole mess."
    – C.D. Wright, *The Book That Jane Wrote: Midnights*

"Man was made for Joy & Woe
And when this we rightly know
Thro the World we safely go
Joy & Woe are woven fine
A Clothing for the soul divine
Under every grief & pine
Runs a joy with silken twine"
    – William Blake, *Auguries of Innocence*

for my family

Contents

I.

II.

III.

I.

To My Insulin Pump

You're part of my anatomy now – port,
they call it. Into the flesh of my belly,
I insert a needle. Needle comes out, but
a tiny plastic capillary remains, affixed
to a button. Buoy on the surface of me.
Black, about the size of an old pager,
I wear you clipped to my bra like a spy.
When delivering insulin, I can hear and feel
a faint *click-whir, click-whir* near my heart,
a cat's purr. Fine plastic tubing runs from
my pump to my button. Somehow
umbilical. It unclasps with a quick twist
if I want a bath. Or to fuck unobstructed.
It would not be exaggerating to say you
(weight of a deck of cards, cost of a small car)
are literally keeping me alive – but I'll just say
you, splendid little engine, are the only part
of me I never find it difficult to love.

A Brief History of the Future Apocalypse

for Chris

Worlds just keep on ending and
ending, ask anybody who survived

an earthquake in an ancient city
its people can't afford to bolt

to the bedrock, or lived to testify
to the tyrant who used his city's roofs

like planks to walk people off,
his country's rivers like alligator pits

he could lever open and drop a whole
angry nation into. Ask anyone

who has watched their own ribs emerge
as hunger pulls them out like a tide,

who watched bloody-sheet-wrapped
bodies from the epidemic burn,

or fled any forever-war.
The year I was eleven, I felt

the ground go airplane turbulent
beneath me. Its curt shuddering

brought down a bridge and a highway
I'd been under just the day before.

And I was not afraid, but should have been
the first time love fell in me like ash.

How could I know it would inter us
both, how could I not? The world

must, I think, keep ending
so long as we keep failing

to heed the simple prophecies of fact –

industry's thick breath fogs our crystal ball,
war is a trapdoor sprung open in the earth

that a whole generation falls through
and love ends, if no one errs, in death.

When my love died, I remember thinking
this happens to people every day,

just – today, it's my world
crashing like an unmanned plane

into the jungle of all I've ever
come to know, but didn't want to.

It feels terrible to feel terrible
and so we let ourselves forget –

Why else would we let the drawbridge
down for a new tyrant, water

the Horseman of Famine's red steed
with the last bucket from the well?

But we forget to give up, too. A heart
sorrow-whipped and cowering

will still nose out to its ribcage
to be petted, will still have an urge

for heroics. And anyway, when has fear
of grief actually kept anyone from harm.

Some hope rustles in my leaves
again. It blows through, they eddy

the floors of me, unsettling
all I tried to learn to settle for.

Would I be wiser to keep
a past sacrament folded in my lap

or would I be more wise to shake
the gathered poppies from my apron,

brush off soft crimson petals
of memory and be un-haunted –

I don't know. So I choose you and we
will have to live this to learn what happens.

And though it's tempting to mistake
for wonders the surge of dappled

white tailed does vaulting through
suburban sliding glass doors,

they are not. Nor vanishing bees
blown out like so many thousands

of tiny candle-flames, neither
the glinting throngs of small black birds

suddenly spiraling out of the sky,
the earth almost not even dimpling

with the soft thuds of feathered weight.
They're not wonders, but signs

and therefore can be read. I didn't
always know that in the ancient Greek

apocalypse

means not the end of the world but
the universe disclosing its knowledge

as the sea is meant to give up its dead,
the big reveal, when the veil blows back

like so many cobwebs amidst the ruins
and all the meaning of all the evidence

will shine in us to finally see –
And there you'll be. And I'll know you

not by the moon in your grin but the song
rung in my animal self. For I feel you,

my sure-handed one, with something
sacreder than instinct but just as fanged.

Then unharness me the way you know
I want so I can watch the stars

blink back on over the garden as we grapple
in the dimming black like little, little gods.

The Woodpecker

Last night at dinner, my husband told the children
the cat had left a red-bristled woodpecker at the door

still heaving her small breast, still blinking a bright eye.
He told them he got his gloves, gently lifted her up,

that she perched for a bit on his finger, frightened
tiny talons gripping and ungripping, until she finally

found her wings and flew off. Did you know, I asked,
this weird fact about woodpecker's tongues? I let

their father explain (because he's the one who told me)
that woodpeckers' tongues wrap around their brains –

a fact so strange and obviously metaphorical it really
deserves its own poem. But this isn't that poem because

a few nights earlier, my husband and I were talking
about poems and he suggested I should really write

a poem about this pandemic we're in. The problem is
I have nothing to say about this pandemic we're in.

If I get sick, I'm one of those people they say it kills.
I saw a political ad in which a lone bed sat in a lone room,

ventilator noises. It said, this is the loneliest death. I
know for a fact there's no such thing as a good death,

only a good life, by which I mean a life spent trying.
Try as I may to wrap my tongue around my brain,

that is all I have to say about this pandemic we're in.
Last night, after we'd put the kids to bed, my husband

told me the truth – the woodpecker, resplendent
in her red, did indeed grip and ungrip his finger,

but she did not (as he told the children) take flight.
She died. In his hands, she let go of her last small breath

and he was left holding this beautiful bird whose song
had gone. I don't know, man, he said, sipping a whiskey,

it really gets to me. I didn't know what to say about that
either, except: It gets to me, too. I thought about

my husband's huge, gentle hands. I thought about
the grace that is trying. How trying is a silent prayer

we all say every day. She died in the hands of someone
who wanted to help. That kind of peace will do.

Spiel: A Love Poem

I wake to find you looking at my belly,
plastic tube affixed to my pale flesh.
My great aunt had it too, you say, innocent
of knowing I've heard this umpteen times.

The plastic tube affixed to my pale flesh
delivers insulin from a device clipped to my bra –
I've rehearsed this explanation umpteen times.
It once surprised a colleague when she hugged me,

the insulin-deliverer clipped to my bra.
I have this spiel I give about the difference
(and gave it to that colleague when she asked me)
between most diabetics, and Type 1s.

In this spiel I give about the difference,
I'm a computer that got programmed wrong.
Not so, most diabetics. Just Type 1.
My body misread my pancreas as hostile, struck

like a computer virus, maybe malware –
Anyway. I no longer have the insulin I need
since the pancreas, blitzed to oblivion, makes that.
I read this story once about the nymph Ondine –

Anyway. The insulin I need is like a courier,
shifting glucose from my blood into my cells.
I'll come back to this story of Ondine, her curse –
No insulin, empty cells. Viscous, jammy blood,

glucose thick in the veins, rusting the capillaries.
When her mortal beloved betrayed her, the nymph
Ondine cursed him: What his body should just do,
like breathe while he sleeps, he would have to choose.

I'm no nymph's mortal beloved, nor betrayer,
but my body no longer does what it just should.
I can breathe while I sleep, but I still have to choose
to keep myself alive each day, to test, to treat

my body that no longer does what it just should.
Ondine's lover, exhausted, simply died. At least
I have a condition I can test, treat, keep myself alive.
In Egypt, in 1552, physician Hesy-Ra noticed ants

drawn to the urine of people exhausted, dying.
Too much sugar in the blood meant death till 1921,
so when in Egypt in 1552 Hesy-Ra noticed people
with nail-polish remover breath, dry heaving

from too much sugar in the blood, death was close.
That thirst so unslakable, anything's like seawater,
that nail-polish remover breath, the dry heaving,
that's ketoacidosis. You pass out, eventually, and die,

but that thirst, so unslakable anything's like seawater,
it could make you beg for death. Low blood sugar,
the opposite of ketoacidosis, also makes you pass out
and maybe die if you don't, as I always do, have Skittles.

Low blood sugar doesn't make you beg for death, but
it makes you shake starting from the hands. Heartstop
maybe within minutes if you don't, as I do, have Skittles
or orange juice or a squeezy honey bear on hand.

I hate that shake, starting from the hands. I fear heartstop,
how fast it can come on. Maybe even while sleeping,
when you don't know you need that squeezy honey bear.
Like Ondine's lover, all I'd have to do to stop is nothing.

It could even happen, I say, while sleeping next to you.
You fumble then, unfastening the pump from me.
All I'd have to do to stop is nothing, but then
I couldn't wake to see you look at me like that.

On Memory

Because today, the leaves of the black walnut tree flicker new season's chartreuse,
Because the pelts of both my cats gleam with the sheen of cherishment,
Because Halloween-cobweb clouds in the blue blue blue blue blue,
Because today, the only thing that aches is my left ring-finger
above the severed wrist tendon bunched inside my palm,
I'm convinced I had an idyllic childhood.

And because today I got a text from an old friend – his accent,
even texting, is sugarcane and Homer and midnight fried fish and long,
shy weariness – and because he said that he's good and his little daughter, also good,
and he can't believe it's been so long since we were last across a cocktail from each other,
the hive whirring in my chest honeys with optimism.

If you asked me on a day one former fall when the moon happened to be sailing between us
and the sun, witching up the afternoon, and a soft-hearted soul told me about my beloved's betrayal,
or if you asked another day in a more recent fall when a fissure in my viscera
made it too painful even to lift the garbage from the bin, let alone walk it to the curb,
I'd tell you all my choices have been disastrous.

But today, if just today, things that were happening seem to have happened.
I am reveling in the first chill's flick to my ear on a long walk, and I'm aware
that my recently broken ribs don't twinge.

Tragedy is everywhere, lurking within the baritone chortle of my friend
whose secret brother has spent his life asleep in a hospital, unfairytaled.
It wafts like scent around my gregarious friend, divorced from a man who woke up one morning
a stranger to them both, left her to miscarry alone on their bathroom floor.

Tragedy cleaves to the one I love, barely a teen when pills melted his father's
heart like a clock –
a perpetual shadow shortening and lengthening
from the place he meets the earth.
But one can only spend so much time inside grief's airless room.

So today (because I can afford to turn up the heat)
I'll shower in plumes of steam, let them veil me in the mirror,
and feel maybe Ovid was right when he said:
Some day this pain will be of use to you.

And maybe it's a trick, a psychological illusion. Disaster will come again,
changing the story by changing its end. Then changing it again.
But today, I can remember a stranger mistaking me for French
at a French bar in New York City, and a quote
painted on the wall there, that said: *Hold me the forgotten way.*
And today, it feels possible to think of that as meaning
love is a thread that can lead us back to the self
at the center of this labyrinth, pawing the dirt with its hoof.

Studies from Childhood

I.

The Grape Arbor

A little girl wakes outside
on a woven polypropylene chaise – yellow
everywhere. In the air,
she tastes baked loam. Beyond
a wide-leafed vine lit with black grapes,
dust-blued, the sky
holds an idea just out of reach.
She looks and looks until she feels everything
turn over, feels herself fall
into the infinite day.

II.

Birch Elevator

Two young conquerors
  with braided hair

caper in the narrow yard.
  One rides in circles, one

in a cut-open cardboard box
  accepts the toll. One conceals

herself amid the star jasmine,
  one seeks. One emerges

squirming off spiders, smelling
  like vernal midnight. One

mounts a board, legs astraddle
  the rope drilled through it.

One pulleys the rope, hoists
  the swing into the white

branches. Okay, one says,
  let me down. Please.

What's the secret word.
  What's the secret word.

III.

Bird of Paradise

Of the flowers in the narrow yard –

snapdragons with soft mouths
you could guppy open between finger
and thumb,

yarrow, sea holly,
Japanese blood grass,
reticent peonies picked open by ants –

the Bird of Paradise was her favorite
because it was not *beautiful*.

Not, like aster, flocked. Nor
aglow with magenta bulbs
like amaranth.

It had none of the helixing wisteria's
clusters of tinkling purple bells.

It seemed to strain
amid the bright clamor, orange

and indigo comb scissored open.
Sometimes she fingered the tapering

green beak, lithe neck, and thought

if *proud* ever looked like anything,
it had to be this.

IV.

Tanbark

The last time she broke her arm –

overreaching, sweaty, her grip slicked
        off the monkey bars –

she landed heart-first
                mouth full of tanbark

mulched throughout the playground.

Sun-flavored redwood. Lumberdust
on the tongue
        The wind knocked out of you,

        a hand making circles on her back
as she gulped for air. Years later,

that moment would bubble up
from the deep aquifer of memory –

                metaphor
upon receiving awful news.

She'd recall her arm's
                wrong, wrong angle

the discordant loveliness of the day

being asked – *1 through 10* –
        how much does it hurt

and finding
        she had nothing to compare it to.

V.

Greased Melon Day

You're a people person,
her mother said
in the voice people use
for wishes.

Blue bathing suit
with a blue ruffle.

The kids in the pool
were trying to get the water-
melon slicked with
petroleum jelly

into mesh-netted
water polo goals.

Diving board end.
Baby pool end.
Go, go play, her mom said.

The kids (all squawk & bleat)
were nice enough but
the greased melon
kept getting and getting

away. End of the day,
she sat in a bath
and cried, watching

slight tears roll
off her oil-glazed arms.

VI.

Bottle Brush Bees

The red-blossomed bush
furred out in the corner
of the narrow yard sizzled
with bees, bristling
cylindrical flowers tipped
with yellow pollen lured
their fuzzy thieves. Once
or maybe twice a month
barefoot she or her sister
might find one, lightning
in the grass; they
devised a whole lexicon
for *sting* – bee-branded,
bumble-shocked, butt-
needled, honey-rung –
despite all their words
what she'll remember is
not how it felt to be stung,
but their constant song.

VII.

Black Mamba

All over the news – bring in
cats, dismantle doghouses,
chicken hutches. Backyard woodpiles

to be avoided, crawlspaces swept
before entering. A threat
called in – illegal pet, most poisonous

snake in the world, gone rogue.
Anti-venom helicoptered in,
blue glow of nightly science

paling all faces. For weeks
nobody felt safe. Who walked
to school was carpooled, under-

run dogs tremble-stretched
on rugs. Announcement:
If it wasn't a hoax, now

there have been enough
slitherless searches, days un-
spotted, successive nights of frost-

crunched lawns. Conclusion:
the snake – if there was a snake –
is gone. The ecstasy of scare,

collective held breath spent,
neighborhood deflated
like balloons cold-shriveled

in a winter room, and fear,
a promise unfulfilled –
worse only than being chased

by real danger: trapped by the lie.
Silence in the narrow yard. All fall
they could have been outside.

VIII.

Lamb's Ear

The sisters' itched-open chicken pox,
       so many cigarette burns –

Okay now, their mother said, unrolling
       a blanket wide in the narrow yard,

stripping both her daughters
       Eden-raw. *It's this or duct tape*

mittens to your hands – her mother
       knew, in mere minutes, sun

would ease their little bodies clenched
       in stress. She watched a blue-black

beetle clamber up a stem. She plucked
       a silver leaf off at its joint

thick, furred Lamb's Ear. She petted
       her sister with its downy pelt.

My turn, said her sister, and she felt
       an instinct yawn a crack into its shell –

a sense that to love well, first
       one might have to get a whiff of hell.

IX.

Juniper Issues

Beside the highway out of town, a massive cement statue of Padre Junípero
Serra kneels, gesturing towards the sea. *Who was he*, she asks through her
reflection in the car window. Her father at the wheel replies, *The one who built
the missions. You had that field trip* – she remembers. Ronald Stamper dared
her to say the f-word and she did, very quietly. And felt wretched. And nobody
heard but God. Later, on the bus, Ronald refused the strawberry Mentos he'd
promised. *No*, he said. *If no-one notices, it doesn't count.* And even then, she
knew that was f-ed up. Pulling in the drive, her father's car gets a hair too close
to the juniper hedge. She hears the branches whine against the door. Her father
turns, grins, *Maybe just don't mention that to Mom?* But first thing that he says
inside: *I scraped that f-ing juniper again,* tousling his perplexed daughter's hair.

X.

Oleander

On the walk to school,
the Screaming House, blade-leaved
oleander menacing through the chain-link fence.

They heard but never saw who howled
wordless, keened. It seemed all day –
Steer clear of there, her mother said. But gloom

beguiles certain minds. And why,
she wondered, wouldn't someone
suffering thus just walk out, harvest

if not the light – the toxic shrub
that hemmed the fetid place. Still there,
hunched in piney darkness, curtains drawn,

oleander bushes in bloom. Last time,
she stood and stood and all she heard –
two daytime owls, lowing in accord.

XI.

Rose Watering

They were in one of many droughts –
if it's yellow let it mellow, shower with a friend –
slogans flourished. The sisters
bucketed out their bathwater
to ransom the narrow yard.
At one end of its crescent, their mother's roses –
sunburn pink, or white and veined
like a bloodshot eye, some the vivid red
of blood in new panties, others

the dark claret of wound.
You water the soil, not the blooms,
or risk black rash spreading
amidst their fleshy petals. She thought
of this as she drained gray suds
delicately onto the roots of a bush
whose fragrant gills flamed orange
as the brushfire thrashing
in the nearby foothills, whose smoke
ghosted the summer wind.

XII.

Sequoia

When she thinks of where she comes from. Fog. Maseca. Estuary birds.
Carolina Duarte made fun of her homemade clothes. The seventh banana slug
on the trail, clinging to an exposed root. Like paint slip. The twelfth. A lemon
tree in the narrow yard. In the narrow yard, dill. Carrots. Sand. Waking one
night after bedtime. Her mother cried, *Because we don't have any goddam money.*
Her father, low voiced. The smell of granite. The dog breathing slow in her
little sleep. The redwoods, softest bark. Soft as rust. Silhouette-colored leaves.
Taller than buildings. Cathedral-columned. So ancient they have names. So
ancient, the origins of their names are a mystery. The shiny black seam where
fire tongued the tree. The square carved out of a trunk so a road could tunnel
through. Bower. Timber. And all those tiny cones that need the fire. It breathes
a spell on them. They split open.

Showing 615 Results for "Diabetes" 12/30/2019–12/30/2021

from a search of The New York Times

When I Googled the word diabetes at 3 in the morning that first scary night, I was completely overwhelmed. She would die without insulin, but too much could kill her. We would have to count the carbohydrates in everything she ate and check her blood sugar constantly.
"It's a terrible, terrible disease," said Dr. Butler at U.C.L.A.
In one study, researchers found that people with diabetes, obesity, hypertension or chronic kidney disease were three times as likely to be hospitalized with Covid-19, regardless of age.
Diabetes felt like an unwanted creature tethered to my beloved child that required its own round-the-clock care.
No one spontaneously gets better.
A French study found 1 in 10 diabetic patients with Covid-19 died within a week of being hospitalized.

"It's a terrible, terrible disease," said Dr. Butler at U.C.L.A.
At least 30 states allow some people with Type 2 diabetes to get vaccines, but only 23 states include people with Type 1 diabetes.
"It feels like many of the prejudices I've fought my whole life I'm fighting all in one bucket to get access to this vaccine," said Jessica von Goeler, 49, of Arlington, Mass., who has Type 1 diabetes.
Living with diabetes puts Ms. Buckley at heightened risk for severe illness if she were to become infected, she said, so she has stopped traveling out of town.
Many of the 300,000 who died from Covid-19 had an underlying health condition, like diabetes.
"It's a terrible, terrible disease," said Dr. Butler at U.C.L.A.
No one spontaneously gets better.
Added to the burden of the disease is the high cost of insulin, whose price has risen each year.
When Caiti Derenze, a lawyer in Jersey City, N.J., went to Walgreens to refill her insulin prescription in July, she was met with a nearly $300 bill.
For chronically ill patients, decisions about whether to pay or go without medications are life-or-death battles that must be fought over and over again.
Ms. Francis isn't sure what she will do. Her age, combined with her diabetes

and high blood pressure, put her at high risk of severe illness if she contracts the coronavirus, which makes her reluctant to take any job that puts her into face-to-face contact with the public.

Dr. Hadjadj added, "You are not the kind of person who can afford to disregard these rules."

One in 10 diabetic patients with Covid-19, the illness caused by the virus, died within a week of being hospitalized, according to a study published on Thursday.

"It's a terrible, terrible disease," said Dr. Butler at U.C.L.A.

Mr. Biden said. "Or, if you have a medical condition like diabetes, or you're a frontline worker like a health care worker or a teacher, you can get a free booster."

"This is a good sign," said Nelson Garcia, 48, who waited more than two hours with his two young children before he was finally within reach of protection from a disease that could be deadly for people with diabetes like himself.

"I have diabetes!" he said, a little too excitedly.

In 6 percent of cases, Covid-19 was the only cause of death. The other 94 percent included underlying conditions such as high blood pressure or diabetes.

"It's a terrible, terrible disease," said Dr. Butler at U.C.L.A.
No one spontaneously gets better.
Diabetes greatly increases their likelihood of having a heart attack or stroke.
It weakens the immune system – one of Dr. Butler's fully vaccinated diabetes patients recently died from Covid-19.

Mr. Safranek had other health problems, including diabetes, but felt assured that even a breakthrough Covid infection would be mild.
"We did everything they told us to," Ms. Safranek said.

He Asks Me to Send Him Some Words (From My House)

Quilt. Skillet. Mat. What it says on the back of that jacket. Teakettle. Key. What I fold. What I flex. My transitive and intransitive agonies. Polish. Peace lily. Spoon. Compassing at. That same tremble. Keep calm and carry on. To lilt. Little bread. The spectacle of longing. Jar. Destinolibro. *Los niños tontos.* And maybe we are but I don't care. Cactus. Couch. To couch in such terms. Revised edition. Lemonade. Fresh mint. *The Complete Nocturnes. The Food of China.* Soap. Glow. My sister at that age. In an empty wine bottle, a dead bee. In an empty coffee cup, a pattern of sediment. In which future. Insulin pump, test strip. Retina. Hemorrhage. Like black ink into a bowl of olive oil. A murmuration of pixels. Baby I may never have, I hold close. Bud vase. Blacken. Balm. Photograph of a woman walking towards. *Cuidados intensivos. The Prelude.* I shine. *La Vita Nuova.* You shine with.

II.

Failing at Epilogue in San Telmo Flea Market

Past rows and rows of glass-glow, every hue
and shade of old-seltzer-bottle blue, down
cobbled streets, curbs banked with downy white
seed-flurry from the tall, leafsome trees that overhang,
past the man who fixes pocketwatches, past the woman
hawking long cables of garlic, there's a silversmith
from whom I bought a thin-banded ring holding one
opalescent oval of pink *rodocrosita*. It's the same stone
out of which the Casa Rosada is blocked and carved,
the grand coral-colored house of government
in front of which Las Madres gathered, garbed in white
in the bad years, holding photos of the disappeared.

I didn't know that when I bought the ring,
placeholder for another given to me by a man I loved
back in a much different future. I do not know
what it's like to lose someone to a despot's terror-
machine, but I do know what it's like to live
with a long, unbroken silence at the end of a hope
that can never be returned. My brain, running
around offleash in my sleep, cannot stop dreaming
he reappears – the sense it makes of a car pulling up
or a door opening elsewhere in the apartment – but
in the dream, he barely knows me, he's not himself
anymore. Much like me. Whatever *me* means now.

The silversmith's table is lined with velvet fingers,
ring-holders flaunting their baubles. It points the way
past the cartoonish mural of a man on a skateboard
in his chullo and sarape, and past the knife sharpener's
whirring kiosk and past the hipster-woodworker
chiseling a curl from the edge of one of his many-
patterned bowls. Past the young woman selling burlap
backpacks and the other young woman selling

plant-pots made from melted vinyl records, drifting
in and out of the scent of sizzling meat, and past
the place where everything is rainbows – flags,
bags, shirts, phone cases – there is a small stall
selling baskets and baskets of antique doorknobs.

One basket is full of beveled crystal prisms, handles
like costume jewelry for the opera. One basket
is a bouquet of brass floral carvings. Here and there,
a doorknob carved like a gargoyle, or carved
like a fist, or carved like a lion's head, or a dog's.
Whatever did you once guard, jowly little demon?
Maybe a nursery, where an infant boy slept soundly
in his white lace dress, or maybe a vaulted office
in which there was a drawer, in which a gun
waited, or perhaps a breezy bedroom where
stealthy lovers fell out of time together, if only
for a sunny afternoon. The least interesting truth,
just because it isn't ours, can captivate the wonderer –

But if I were to twist the neck of the toothy beast,
would I find a young violinist repeating arpeggios,
a seamstress bent over a wedding dress that will
never be worn, a writer of poems still unpublished,
a general smoking a black cigarette? If I could
turn every handle in the basket, what would
open? Looking for answers, I keep turning up
more questions. How foolish have I been, to imagine
that what I opened, I could choose not to enter –
to imagine what I opened, I could ever close again.

Chronic Illness Imagined as a Haunting

Origin of most of my chaos, ghost
       hiding between the walls
of my cells   flickering the lights

            the way a heart
stutters through a panic attack.

Since I'm eleven years old, constant
       daily annoyances –

         It's forever stalling or else
speeding up the clocks, fucking with

my sense of time, the way ten minutes
       means something different

if you're furrowed over a new
      recipe for béchamel
            or waiting
      for an ambulance.

Little things that, dementor-esque,
       siphon off the life force:

Middle of the night, it shakes me awake
     from the inside, or,
          because I'm hurrying

to a first day of teaching,
       it'll hide all my test strips,
    knowing that I cannot go without.

Like a poltergeist that'll steal the ace
        from a full deck of cards
                        just to make it useless,

my ghost has a thousand ways
                to ruin all the fun.

        Blood sugar too high for a beer
on the brewery tour,
                not a bite of the towering
        carrot cake at my sister's wedding.

A miniscule crack in the insulin pump
        lets just a tear's-worth of sea water in,
so it fails while we're snorkeling

in Key West. It keeps beeping, beeping

on a boat full of sun-honeyed tourists
        wondering what is that noise –

                can't have any of the tropical
fruit plattered out in concentric crescents.

Can't get back to land (to fix this)   any faster
                than the captain is willing to go.

All the things you do to appease it –
        not leaving a heel of bread on a sill
                or passing the videotape along,

but pricking my finger to draw a seed of blood,
                        plant it on a plastic strip –

        Sometimes
I leave those around for my ghost to find.

Still, still   the ever-present sense of threat.

That it's loosening the blades
      of the ceiling fan thumping in my chest,

doing its best to imbalance the bookshelves
of my hormones
      I'll one day be found pinned under.

Or it'll push me down the staircase
        of a low blood sugar and I'll
      end up rag-dolled at the bottom.

Knowing it's hell-bent on my betrayal
       I recite my lists of ways
          that I might die,

which I'm always working on
      so I can ghost-proof against them:

Could it fuck with the caulk, cause a leak,
      moisten a joist so my bathtub-shaped
kidney falls?

That kind of insipid long-term shit
         is just its style.

To anticipate it, I have detectors
       everywhere –

Smoke, yes, and carbon monoxide, like everyone
      but also devices
       bespoke to my harassment.

A device to measure the rise and fall
       of sugars in the body, another

to deliver the life-saving potion
that keeps the ghost in the blood quiet,
                        still another that just

        makes the sound of a woman's voice

if I haven't spoken for awhile,
                        so I can haunt it back.

Andean Pastoral

What's left of an Incan wall
doilied by lichen – a place
once made then unmade.
Sacred. Grass expanse,
trumpeting cacti, trampled
petals of boneset. Slowly
I vanish into everything:
wedged stones, lizards plumping
in the sun, wind unspooling
in the lower field. I thought
I would feel sadder but
I just feel ghostless.
A little godfooted mouse
emerges. The world holds
itself somehow unimaginably
together. A black-winged bird
flares in the neglected arbor.

Ode to Anthony Bourdain

"As you move through this life and this world you change things slightly, you leave marks behind, however small. And in return, life – and travel – leaves marks on you. Most of the time, those marks – on your body or on your heart – are beautiful. Often, though, they hurt."
    – Anthony Bourdain

I'm sitting on my couch watching a man on TV
get a tattoo symbolizing *epoché*, a Pyhronnic skeptic's term

meaning *to suspend judgement*, or as Montaigne translated,
to hold back. The man on the TV mentions Plato's assertion –

All I know is that I know nothing. It does not strike me that
either Plato or Tony Bourdain knows nothing. Maybe

because they know more than me. The man on the TV
tells me that he doesn't really know who he is – no longer

a chef, not really a journalist, maybe (he says) he fancies
himself an essayist. Good. Essayists don't actually have to

know anything; *to essai* – in French it means to try, as in,
to attempt, but also, to test, to taste, perhaps for the first time,

a gleaming heap of tofu cubes doused in a red shiny
ground pork gravy, strewn with bias-sliced scallions. *Mapo Dofu,*

Bourdain says, *is everything you want in your mouth, in one perfect bite.*
The goal of Pyhronnic skepticism is to arrive at *ataraxis,*

a kind of Western Nirvana – this tall man on the TV says
it means *to be unperturbed, happy in your life, not*

tormented. But who among us is not, somehow, tormented?
Plato, who said he knew nothing, also said: *Be kind*

for everyone you meet is fighting a hard battle. I know less
than nothing, but I know that to be true. The man on TV

raises a glass of beer to his companion, who relates
the story of his infancy in Ethiopia, the tuberculosis

epidemic, how his ailing mother walked her two sick kids
seventy-five miles to the Swedish hospital, how she died

and he and his sister ended up in Stockholm – and then
the food comes, a vast expanse of spongy injera bread

islanded with kitfo (beef tartare blessed with hot chili)
and collard greens, doro wat (chicken stewed with eggs),

yellow lentils, carrots, and little bright vermillion mounds
of berbere spice. It's a painter's palate of delights, eaten

with the hands, as intimate and visceral as it gets, and
as they tuck injera-pinched lamb tibs into their mouths,

they close their eyes in a gesture that in every language
means, *This pleases me so much.* But pleasure is not

happiness. If anything, it's closer to – what? Oblivion,
I think. (Though thinking is not knowing.) Escape.

To please the body is to distract the mind from all
its striving after knowing, all it's wheeling dread. Wine,

wonder, sex, song. And food – the slow-motion ooze
of baked Camembert from its broken crust, the gratifying

crackle of a fork through the edge of well-crisped Tahdeeg,
the exquisite tang of a hand-whipped aioli barely flecked

with fresh dill, noodles slurped out of a steaming broth
afloat with bright green herbs, the way pit-barbequed pig

just unfetters itself in the pit-master's great gloved hand.
Now Tony Bourdain is saying, about a nation to which he

is newly arrived, *You might not know this place is so lush,
so often have we seen its name thrown up across a dusty*

famine scene. What we think we know. How impoverished
our imaginations can be. How easy it is, to misunderstand

a man, or a woman, or a people. The man on TV, because
he is on TV, feels like a friend to me. He eats the same

Trippa alla Romana I couldn't quite bring myself to swallow
when I was in that same terra cotta city. He alludes

to his misspent youth, and I feel a surge of recognition
that washes some of my own regrets out to a further shore.

Perhaps I, too, will one day make it to Jerusalem. Maybe I
will get to recount to someone, across a smooth black table

lit by a single Edison bulb, my own version of his story
in which I am the one taken aback by sudden splendor.

Once, in Hungary, I ate the perfect dinner – velvety
pale green cream of celery soup pebbled with bleu cheese,

flaked with crisp bacon, then goose leg roasted
to a delicate crackle, daubed with demi-glace, then
sour cherries dark, round like a word in another tongue

you love the sound of but cannot quite pronounce, all
while sipping a silky wine called Bull's Blood, grown

and stomped just paces from where we were eating.
My sister took one bite and sighed, *Dear. People. Of Earth* –

an invitation. An ode. I love this man on the TV, in a TV way,
and that's a paradox. He is hidden in plain sight, where people

feel they know what they haven't thought to wonder after.
Most of us, after all, do not have an *epoché* tattoo, do not

suspend judgment, hold back. Don't always try. And
don't always understand why one might seek the oblivion

of pleasure, or of watching others live their lives in public,
or even of death. There is another word the Ancient Greek

skeptics sometimes used – *acatalepsy*. It means, the in-
comprehensibility of things. Now Bourdain says, *I want*

to explore an African nation that was never colonized. And now,
after the phone rang and I missed some stuff, he is

saying he doesn't think another tattoo will make him hipper, or
more relevant, or interesting. He is tall, snowy, has

some lank to him. And he's dead now. And now, he says,
forever and ever, *It's been an adventure.* He says, *We took*

some casualties over the years. Things got broken. Things
got lost. But I wouldn't have missed it for the world.

Sacsayhuamán

Human-hewn masterpiece
of mountain stones, it is
massive. There's no other
word for it. Fortress, temple,
monument to the technology
of its Incan architects. Alfredo
jokes its name is pronounced
like *sexy womán*. It is sexy

if, like me, you're drawn to
rune, to the sublime. Subtlety
has never really been my thing –
I swoon for the scale of all this.
We're at 11,000 or so feet
altitude. I'm not falling asleep,
I'm plummeting, that feeling
the world has trap-doored
beneath you. I knock over
a lamp, grabbing the nightstand

to keep from black-holing down.
I wake with blood in my eye.
Chronic disease, not that sexy
but I won't let it keep me
from clambering these ramparts.
Not when I've come this far.
The mortarless rhomboid rocks
almost fused, cellular, make shapes –
the puma's paw, the guinea pig.
A three-tiered altar. A reservoir
long bereft of lake. And a door
opening onto the thin, cold clouds.

Imaginary Prisons

after the etchings of Giovanni Battista Piranesi

What knowing constructs the ramparts of the mind?
      Once, asked when (if had I the great and terrible engine

of a history-hopping device) I would ferry myself,
      all I could think was – history is no place

for the likes of me. Where among the arched and columned
      halls of the Palatine Hill would I find syringes?

For all that green marble, for all those chiseled marble veils
      and sinews, what I require to survive is nowhere

that side of refrigeration. And still scarce, anywhere
      without. No matter how my brain has ached with wonder

to gaze upon the starry domes and tessellated mezzanines
      of caliphate Damascus, to swoon in its jasmine-bedecked

arbors, there is no prayer that could bear me up, there. Or anywhere
      after the future failures of infrastructure, marking

the Anthropocene's demise. I have no nostalgia for the next
      zombie apocalypse, a world so well-imagined on TV,

throbbing with violence. Scene set for survival of the most
      ruthless, trauma-inured bands of hale survivors

battling it out among the death-flensed stumblers.
      Off I'd go to root for unlooted insulin in a flickering

pharmacy or hospital somewhere. I'll be right back,
      even unsaid aloud, a thought to scrimshaw my fate

into tooth and bone. Fantasies, yes, like the Great Wheel
　　　　　or the Round Tower or the Drawbridge of Piranesi,

invented dungeons he etched to hold-fast secret fears.
　　　　　He may not have drawn his own face on the man

racked beneath an ominous garland of chains but
　　　　　it's somehow human nature to seek ourselves

in many horrors, to test our sense of belonging against
　　　　　the story of another's, be it myth or rumor

or reassembled fragments of history – that shattered bowl
　　　　　whose missing pieces make it impossible

to complete. I have wondered, what would the child
　　　　　who died (as I would have) by twelve have become

if not for our disease? Or if they had the medicine
　　　　　sooner, always. Would they have invented the glass

bridge, or a new way of cooking thistle? Or would they,
　　　　　like Piranesi, like me, sit for hours illustrating our ruins

real and imagined, as if recreating them over and over
　　　　　would somehow, someday, render them intact –

Reverse-Engineering Their Sacrifice

Mummy with a collar of marigolds. Mummy resting his chin on his hands. Sneering mummy. Sleeping mummy. Mummy with salt from the Incan mines at Maras still on her lips. How did you make your ends? Burlap-wrapped mummy, cinched with ropes. Mummy swaddled in brightly-striped blankets. Mummy with a single round hole in his skull. Mountainslide mummy. Rock-hive mummy, lakeshore mummy. Mummy found above cloudcover. Fetal-curved, dove-toed. Mummy wearing a feathered headdress. Mummy wearing a silver brooch. Mummy with blood on his cap. Mummy sitting criss-cross. Broken mummy. Gone mummy, grave-robbed. Mummy wearing an alpaca cape. Lightning-struck mummy. (What do you prove?) Maiden mummy. Mummy whose CT scan shows optical nerves intact. Many-braided mummy. Bronze-braceleted mummy. Mummy sent to his death with a doll. Mummy found with her own umbilical cord in her hands. (Why did they save it? What did they know?) Heavy mummy, full of ice. Mummy with pleated skin. Perfect mummy, who looks like my friend Jaime. Mummy whose CT scan shows a lump of chewing coca in her mouth. Baby mummy with an elongated skull. Mummy separated from her children. Mummy with a manicure. Mummy who looks and looks at nothing. Whose black hair lights the wall.

At Teufelsberg in the Subjunctive Mood

The subjunctive is not a tense
       but a mood – uncertain, wishful,   regretful.

I wish   I spoke his language
      better.   We reach
through a haze   of no-shared native tongue –
      in his cottony accent, he tells me
how they came here   as teens,
      built fires,
          smoked pot,   got a little
drunk, ran from the *Polizei*,   clattered
bikes   down the hill's
      narrow gullies,   youth
          chronicled in shiny hieroglyphs
      on knee   cheek   palm.

  Subjunctive forms   can indicate
        states of unreality.

We conjugate our anecdotes this way –
      If   that ad for a language party
had been correct.   If it hadn't been
raining.   If not for that hot toddy.
      If not for my homesickness,   the fire
pawing at its glass oven door.
         If his friend hadn't caught a cold.   If
      the river hadn't been running over
and   over   the stars reflected there,
      like so many tiny bright stones. Perhaps
      we would not now be arriving
in the Grünewald by train,   to climb a hill
      built of the rubble Berlin had been
      blasted into   by war's end –

Today, the many steps
          are matrixed with frost.
     Teufelsberg   Devil's Hill,
          the highest point
in Berlin –   from here, I can see the Allianz
building at Treptower Park,
          at Alexanderplatz   the Fernsehturm,
slender tack   pinned at the center
     of the city's map,   silver divots
of its sphere   refracting pale spring sun.

Tense refers to when an action takes place:
     past, present, future.

     History resists
the subjunctive,   petrified   into a sense
     of the inevitable.   But what if
          the Russians   had showed their soldiers
some humanity in Stalingrad?   Not two men
          or more to each gun, the unarmed
hoping for a comrade's death,   bequest
of a weapon –   just more bodies,
     Khrushchev schemed, than the Germans
                    had men or metal to kill.
     They might never have
made it here, or won   the Battle of Berlin,
     forced Hoschi's grandmother
          into labor as a *Trümmerfrau*,
                    Rubble Woman
 who trucked   and barrowed the collapse
          here,   dumped first
          in the right-angled courtyard
of Hitler's military college,   then
     amassing.   What if,
          the dragon. What if, its lair.

When used in English, subjuctive forms   frequently
      occur in subordinate clauses,   that-clauses
                                    such as
I suggest that   you be careful, or   It is important that
      you remember where you come from.

Where I come from,   the sea
      runs aground against the mountains –
the reedy baylands   rinsed cool with fog
            but the air   of the sun-cured foothills
                              ghostlessly wild.
But we're here now,   peering through a fence
            by now just grafts of other fence
                  and tinny junk   and weeds
behind which   the geodesic radomes
      of the American spy station, like
                  great white compound eyes, gaze blankly
from their tinker-toy columns
            whose tattered white cloth walls –
                  thin enough to let the voices through –
      fill like sails   then slacken
Hoschi doesn't say,
            "That reminds me," but
                  translating too literally
from German,   "That remembers me."

Subjunctive forms of verbs   might also
            express how a speaker   feels
 about the action described.

                              I wish
we had brought our bolt-cutters.   I wish
      we'd brought some beers. I wish
            these vines, stiff,   in places
as thick as my wrist,   were not covered
      in small spines. I wish the path
            were not so crumbly, I keep grasping

60

handfuls of thorns   to stop from sliding
into the slim birches below.   I wish
        I didn't have to worry
            about my blood sugar
   when I'm far from the nearest kiosk
selling Coke   and cigarettes,
     newspapers and chocolate bars
       and those airplane-sized bottles
of vodka and Jagermeister,   but I can feel
I'm getting low.
           We find a clearing.
Hoschi surveys the snarl of brambles,
     the ruined towers looming there.
  "In English,   how do you call
the fairy tale   where the girl sleeps
    for a hundred years?"   I look up,
     "Sleeping Beauty?"   But not
spindles or princes – cement walls
     and razor wire and the long, slow sleep
       of reason.
           I prick my finger
to test my blood.   A red drop
   trembles on the whorl of a pin-
     pocked fingerprint.

*   The subjunctive*
   can be used to formulate   a hypothetical,
an imagined possibility,   an alternate
         past, obligation, or
 an action   that has not yet occurred.

Who might   I be now, if I'd never had
   that one childhood day   a doctor said, "Yes,
for the rest of your life."
   Would I still have trouble taking things
for granted?

Would that I could see
without thinking,   "There is no blood
            purling in my eyes today."
                                            But then,
        would I still have wanted to know
                    how stories work,
            why she cuts off her heel,   eats the poison
apple, unseams the wolf,   the ones
                that let us see in the dark?   Mirror,
        mirror,   on the wall.   Music comes
from the other   side of the mangled fence
            so there must be a way –
                            yes. Past
            the docile Rottweiler
        and the rebar arranged such that
it must be meant as art,   handkerchiefs
                                            knotted about,
                    a spray-painted stencil
        of a gas mask, a mural   of a nude woman
rendered in many colors.
                We climb the lightless stairwells
                    to the tower's faceted dome
where suddenly
                                it's very quiet.
I point my phone   at the ground,
            click a picture of my long shadow
        in the doorway.   I wonder   if my children
will speak a native language   I never
quite   master.   I take another photo
        of an airplane flying low. I wonder
                                if I want that.

The subjunctive is somewhat rarely used
        in English.   But in other idioms, such as
Spanish,   or German, one's fluency
                    might almost be measured
by one's comfort   *with those forms.*

I am learning   a new language
        for curiosity, for qualm,
                                catching sense
in snippets,   as listeners
        in this tower would have done,   spying
on my own   intuitions.
        A single folding chair   faces out
                where a wall   would have been.
Nobody   seems to have sat there
                        for awhile. I settle
slowly,   eavesdropping on me
        as I flutter through these phrases
                lifted   from my lessons –
I wonder and *I wonder* and   *I doubt*
        and   *Were I to become*   and *Maybe*
that would mean   and *Would*
        that it were so and   *I always imagined*
I might and   *What if we could* and *How*
would we ever   and   *Would you* and
        Would I and   *Would that I were* and   *If*
only   and *I'm sorry but*   and

                Would that I could stay.

Blood Magic

I'm diabetic because my great-great-grandfather was a goat thief, or fell in love with the wrong daughter, or left the healer-woman's debt unpaid.
I'm diabetic because I was arrogant as a child.
Or I'm diabetic because someone, somewhere, prayed to the wrong idol.
I'm actually diabetic because my immune system attacked my pancreas and mash-potatoed it.
But at one time, I was convinced I'm diabetic because Caroline cursed me in the third grade, when I wouldn't sleep over at her house.
Perhaps I'm diabetic because someone, somewhere, way back when, was a harlot.
Perhaps I'm still diabetic because I didn't walk barefoot the cairn-teetered paths of Croagh Patrick.
Or because I didn't believe the hippie at the airport who told me sprouted grains would fix it.
I'm diabetic because as a child I read comic books on the toilet.
No, I'm diabetic because as a child I was infected with a virus that mutated my immune system.
I'm diabetic because: recessive genes.
I'm not diabetic because Yaya failed to keep the right gilded, incensed, red-becandled shrine.
I'm not diabetic because Papou left his bread at the threshold of the wrong mausoleum.
But I am diabetic, in part, because in January, 1922, a fourteen-year-old boy dying of diabetes in a Toronto hospital was given the first ever human dose of insulin.
Insulin from cattle, which earned Banting and Macleod a Nobel Prize.
If not for that, those eldritch sciences, I wouldn't be diabetic. I wouldn't be at all.

The Beelitz Heilstätten

an abandoned hospital complex in what was formerly East Germany

Through the hazy windows
of the gilded sanitorium
a grand staircase rises, iced
with dashed stained glass.
An old cage elevator

fogged with cobwebs
rusts in a dim corner.
Around this compound
palatial wrecks decay –

a strange necropolis.
Someone spray-painted
WHITE POWER
in black on a brick wall,
the O in POWER, a smiley face.

I have a knife
I am only aware of
when we see other people –
they're like us, just

prospecting these ruins.
Or they are not like us but
we assume like us.
With a knife.

Hoschi jokes, Don't be
such a Soft Egg or Warm-
Showerer or One Who Slows Down
at a Yellow Light – German
has many words for wimp.

The haunt-handled shutters
on the operating theater
bang loudly in the wind.
In all the stairwells,

graffiti – cyan, yellow,
black, red. M+C, J+S,
Die Nazi Scum.

Come spring,
the reddest small strawberries
at the Wochenmarkt
will come from these woods.
And the white asparagus –

as it peeks its nose out,
they bury it again, so
it never sun-toughens green.
Soft, fat, sweet. And white
as a blind cave salamander.

We leaf-shuffle through
to the women's ward.
A filigree of roots
fringes the edge
of the Frauenhaus roof
gripped by many delicate trees;

vines have softly picked
all the windows open
and through them,
gusts of birdsong.

Another German word
for wimp is *Frauen-
versteher*. Woman-
understander.

Inside, the Frauen Haus
is dim. Cathedral-vaulted.
An owl lows in the rafters.

My sister texts from
six hours behind to say
she's making my recipe
for fish tacos and how much
exactly is a fuckton
of cilantro. The ping echoes.

It's sunny in her latitude
today. She's drinking
a gin-tonic but I am not
supposed to tell.

Tell who? The distance
between us vibrates
with immensity.

Here, the stone angels
are Fibonacci-ed with frost.
The glow-wine will be out
at the Stadtbahnhof when we
return, and there's this tang
in the air that means snow.

Drinking at Szimpla with Emily and Laurel

"Only those who are belated can observe a ruined form."
    – Susan Stewart, *The Ruins Lesson*

We're sipping beers on the backseats
                from a defunct East German Trabi

in the plant-addled courtyard of an old factory
         in the Jewish Quarter of Budapest

and trying to elevator-pitch this "ruins-pub" to each other.

– reclaimed, industrial-chic warehouse meets
        herbology class or   *a vintage shop (vinyls,*

old street signs, mismatched porch furniture under
        a cataract-cloudy chandelier)

meets community garden –

What is it   about ruins

      that lures
Romantic poets to the ancient forum,
        tourists like us to gin joints like this?

Something about (it's happening right now)
               the cognitive dissonance
        of a punk rock song
     playing   on an ancient gramophone,

the curious simultaneity
               of collapsed binaries
        causing you to briefly stop
      taking either term for granted –

Or reminders of people who went through hell
                    by keeping going,

evidence of   continuity, some
          unpretentious history just   existing –
a spatial archive.

Maybe, we muse, it's as simple   as the juxtaposition
                    of a long white dress
                        and a rusted I-beam,

or a clamber of vines up   rebar, wrought iron –

like the pleasure of what two terms of a metaphor
                        can do to each other.
But this place is not a metaphor,

I'm sitting in the middle of the fact of it.

Em and Laurel continue to discuss
          while I slip into a thought not mine, hearing
      Radnoti's final lines,
And that's how you'll end too

          Last words written in watery ink
on pages found crumpled in his coat pocket:

      Patience flowers into death now.

Poetry has a long memory. It knows
                how quickly, with what ease
the boots come back.

This afternoon   we're in a hip bar
                we imagine will collapse soon enough
          under the weight of its own coolness,
and this era of decadence,

                                its masquerades
        and market days, exhibits, shows,
                orange afternoon beers may all go.

While we cheers in a language not our own,

elsewhere, the edges of a founding document
        frizzle and smoke in its protective display;

when politicians walk past,
                                a sound like cracking ice.

                Electronic music comes on upstairs
        and I can hear in it
the distant sirens   of an old doom.

But looking around
                at this baroque concrete exoskeleton

I find myself thinking,
                        it's not only the boots
                                that can come back
but also what they trampled –

lights in the labs flicker on again,
        banned books reappear on library shelves,

                someone sweeps up while someone else
straightens paintings   on the gallery wall

and a pub opens
                        where a factory used to be

and people can go there and think   perhaps wrongly
        about what survives.

Sligo Abbey

While I grew in my mother's womb, a tumor
grew on her larynx – a stone in her throat
she could not sing out. From then

my shadow wore these small black wings
my shoulders could sense, but not flex –
a feel for threat. Radiation

fused my mother's vocal chords. For months
at a time, she couldn't speak except
by sign, or by a kind of clapping code –

syllables of emphasis compressed
between her palms – [clap CLAP clap] for my name,
for Emily [CLAP clap clap]. *I hate it*

she says of the only voice I've ever known
her to hum. The guide asks my mother
if she's got a cold. Though it's been thirty years,

my mother blushes. *Cholera*, the guide explains,
swept through this part of Ireland
many times. The Abbey was a ruin

by 1641, but since you cannot unbless
consecrated ground, soul-panicked families
barrowed their splotched bodies here

and banked earth over them, mounding it.
You can see, here the guide gestures
towards a stone arch, peak barely a few feet

higher than the thick viridian lawn,
the Abbey didn't sink, as it might seem,
rather, the ground swelled with the dead –

a bone tide, rising. I look down at my feet
beneath which I divine a clatter
of femur and ulna and socket and skull.

They didn't really understand the symptoms
the guide leads us along the cloister's colonnade,
and in the rush to stave infection, sometimes

people were laid into makeshift catacombs alive.
One young woman's journal from that time
describes the victims, sallow and blood-eyed,

knuckles black-raw from clawing their way
out of mass graves, staggering
from the Abbey, vomiting dirt and bile.

That young woman, she smiles fondly,
went on to become Bram Stoker's mom.
My mother rises with her camera

from an eroding relief of winged skeletons
and says, in a voice someone else might hear
as stretched tight with feeling, *I bet you'll end up writing*

this down. And I say, *O, probably.* Wondering
if I can write as far down as it takes
to find where the living are buried.

Ohio

"The American economy runs on poverty, or at least the constant threat of it...the barest glimmer of worker power is treated as a policy emergency, and the whip of poverty, not the lure of higher wages...the appropriate response."
    – Ezra Klein, *The New York Times*

Before they tore down   the abandoned mall,
a journalist photographed the ruination –

fondant snow on the stilled escalators,

shattered shopfront glass, trees and grasses
overtaking the food court, elevator shaft.

In the many-creviced parking lot,

a turmoil of weeds. Police arrested a man
for taking up residence in a vacant store.

Elsewhere, a body, victim of a grim intent.

It'll be an Amazon fulfillment center soon.
A few hours away, what remains of Utopia

(a general store run by an emphazemic couple,

a sagging barn, an underground church
built by the Spiritualists who almost all died

in the 1847 flood) is a Midwest manifestation

of a dread setting in everywhere. Each day,
harder to earn the rent, each summer

sears hotter, each year medicine siphons

more scarce wages away. Nothing else
changes. Hope is a nest on a brittle branch

in a be-nettled field. People turn on each other,

brawl-mongering, grappling for scraps or
any villain to un-hat. I've felt fragile

for awhile now. Second year of grad school,
my university ended our health insurance.

I looked into buying but. Pre-existing condition.

It seemed I was being told, A body like yours
has too many needs for the life of the mind.

I felt like a sapling weighed down with kudzu.

My folks tried to help. I chose to go without
an insulin pump, rationed my medications –

The kudzu crept into my retinas. But

I still read. Villon, Clare, Margery Kempe
who wept perpetually for the world. Later,

I'd find myself in Cincinnati, pointing out

to my own graduate student, a large mural
next to a boarded up row house on a street

eye-patched with plywood, hatch-battened.

Not long before, she whispered me her new
diagnosis. Dream-defeating, she worried.

I think what I said was, You belong here.

We admire the blackwhite over red brick mural:
Racoon under possum under squirrel.

They seem to be sleeping so soundly,
our tenacious creatures, heaped furrily up the wall

of a city that doesn't want them around.

I Ask Him to Send Me Some Words (Reading *The Florida Handbook*)

He sends me: Limestone. Manatee bones. Onyx. He sends me: Rills. (I look this up. Small streams.) He sends me: Venice. He sends me: Honeycombed with caves. He sends me: Sard (I look this up: A yellowish form of chalcedony. I look that up: Microcrystalline quartz.) He sends me: Citrus. Carnelian, like Sard but darker, deep redder. He sends me: Kissimmee. Suwanee. Nassau. All the harbors of the world. He sends me: Merely a shoal in the Pamlico Sea. He sends me the names of streams: Botheration. Whiskey George. (Gorge? No, George. So sayeth the handbook.) He sends me: Fiddlestring Bay. He sends me: California Creek may have first been Califonee, which translates as "home camp." This, he says, he picked especially for me. My home camp. He sends me: Redneck Riveria. This, I think, he picked especially for him. He is not a redneck but he could have been. His home camp. He sends me: Flowstones and draperies. He sends me: Ilmenite. Pleistocene. He sends me: Going for a coffee refill and a Pop-tart. I say: Pop-tart. I think of teen girl singers. I say: You're a Pop-tart. He sends me: Emerald Coast. He sends me: Miracle Strip. I say: Miracle Strip? It sounds like a sexy dance. And I would blush to tell you now the manner of his reply.

III.

Discourses of Diabetes Care

It all starts with the language of *control* – that complicated concept, our north
pole. As if a sport or workout, they'll talk *goals,* scroll through your *machine*
for testing blood. To know you're in control, you have to *test*. Like school, those
who *comply* perform best. Like church, there's guilt, or sometimes getting
blessed by nurses who then call your vitals: Good. The doctor waits for you
to be confessed. A nurse once told me I was being tested. She slid the needle
in my arm-crook, rested while my blood throbbed darkly into vials. God, she
offered, wouldn't send me trials I was not prepared for – that felt wrong. But
then again, I've always been headstrong. The thing is, death and violence ever
hover: like soldiers we should *follow the regime*, hollowed out by harrowing
routine. We *shoot* for our blood sugar's *target range*. We cock the *lancet*, sounds
like guns or spears. We numb a little – all these words, just there – you take
your *shots*, you get your *jabs* – that's *care*. Don't argue – you'll be proved first
wrong, then wronger. And what doesn't kill you just lasts longer. That's how
complications work, it's simple: submit, or you can suffer by example. It's hard
enough to understand the score, the kind of body-horror that's in store for you
if you ignore the basic rules. (A doctor once described such folks as "fools.")
These words of judgement hurt - sometimes, I cry. Sometimes, I hemorrhage
inside the eye, see red, then black - corn syrup glowing down a camera lens.
Then fade out. Here's a noun: Cost: Of doing business, cost of living. This is the
thing that might smart most of all – the cost of insulin can take its toll. As in,
for whom the bell. We pay steep rent to dwell in our own bodies (what percent
increase should be enough from year to year?) They say, "small price to pay"
– that's hard to hear. Suggesting that "you get what you deserve"? That would
hit a neuropathic nerve. Control, control. Who's in control of what? It doesn't
feel like me, deep in my gut. We're pinholes in the blackout shade, unrolled –
numbers made of numbers, truth be sold. I sigh, I fold my hands. I never learn.
It sucks to smolder at these things I cannot spurn.

Our Splendid Failure to Do the Impossible

"All of us have failed to match our dream of perfection. I rate us on the basis of our splendid failure to do the impossible..."
　　　　　– William Faulkner, in a *Paris Review* interview, New York City, 1956

1.

Diagnosis

She shifts on the vinyl exam table
aware of its butcher paper
on the backs of her bare thighs.

In the corner, her mother weeps
into a chrysanthemum of tissues.
The doctor has just said, in the voice

people use for spooked horses,
perfectly normal life. Then says, *perfect control*.
She's so relieved she's not going to die.

To her, the doctor says, *Pretty soon
it'll be just like tying your shoes*. She looks
at her dirty Keds. Neon pink laces.

At home, her mother gives her
a tuna fish sandwich, fizzy
orange drink. She has no idea

she's just been poured her own heap
of seeds to sort, no helper ants.
She's grateful not to be thirsty.

2.

Clockwork Girl

There is inside me
a stopped clock, wind-up
doll stalled at the stroke
of twelve – my first cakeless
birthday, first taste of grief
for a little self uncandled
by a diagnosis, a morning
I learned I would
spend the rest of my days
saving my life. A selfie
shows gray hair now, sun-
spots on my neck, crinkles
around my knees. Wedding
photos show a woman
in a white crepe gown
doubling down on forever,
ring finger a lever pulled
to spin cherries and sevens
and cartoon hearts
through her eyes. But
in the looking glass, I
gaze back perpetually at a girl,
chin-zits and blond flyaways
and sneakers with so many
multi-colored shoelaces,
whose future never happened –
this other one did. And it's
a fine future so far. But
each year, cutting a thick slice
of leopard-crusted pizza or
ruffly quiche, I think
(without really thinking
about it) of that key
in my back, that won't turn.

3.

Notes on the Impossible

What a remarkable burden, to see in every block of lavender-veined Carrara marble a body caught, yearning to be loosed. No lifetime could release them all. But like being in love, the point is not to finish the job. We listen through long silences. We lick each other's wounds the ways we know will please. We gather soft fur from the lint trap to nest a downed bird. And just as those sandbagging the cathedral know the ache in their shoulders will not slow the war, just as the fisherman netting Coke bottles out of the estuary knows there will not be fewer next week, just as the nurse knows her soft sponge wets the lips of a dying man, there is grace in every gesture of ongoing. I will never be better, but I am already older than an age I once prayed to make. My insulin pump buzzes between my breasts. I take what it tells me to.

4.

The Impossible Body

The impossible body is so beautiful
it is grotesque –

cheekbones like airplane wings,
petal-soft skin, bedimpled smile.

A bottom like two cantaloupes
nestled in a gunnysack, lustrous

shoulders, and fingernails shaped
exactly like almonds. Every organ

of the impossible body works
just the way it's supposed to –

you can practically hear its spleen
purr. If you ask the impossible

body, it will run the Inca trail. If
you ask it to open its legs,

it will bloom like a headlight
nearing your rearview mirror.

The impossible body has never,
ever had a fever, or a sunburn, or

a cat scratch. The impossible body
has never sprained an ankle

rolling off a platform heel.
The impossible body doesn't know

that it's impossible. It just keeps
swimming the shark-traffic

of the channel. In fact
the only thing the impossible

body could never figure out
how to do is just, exist.

5.

How the First of Many Burnouts Begins

They teach me to shoot up
on an orange, vesicles rendered
opulent with saline, I learn
the pungent scent of insulin,
elixir of Band-Aid and animal,
how to stick my fingertip
for a bead of sugared blood...

Like the doctor said, like tying your shoes...

I know I'm supposed to be
in control – or else – but cannot
remember if anyone actually
came out and said: If you aren't
perfect, your body will become a hell
of your own making, a cell where you
deserve to rot. And it'll be nobody's fault
but your own...

Yet it was there, somehow, all the time...

Now a teen, I sit on a closed toilet
in a bathroom stall at Chili's
holding a drawn syringe I cannot
bring myself to dart into my thigh
as I'd done by now a thousand times...

Like a kind of aphasia, I know...
But I cannot...

And I know I cannot not...

Eventually I ping, ping my flesh
with the needlepoint until finally
I find a numbish spot
and stinger it gently in...

Are you okay, they ask at the table
and I say yes
and eat the food now cold...

6.

Short Essay on Failure

When they cut my uncle open for his kidney transplant, they found his heart was a cracked egg nested among petrifying vessels. The transplant took, but they sent him home in hospice. My mother said, sadness a garrote around her throat: He never took care of himself.

Only with this disease that runs in my uncle's and my corrupted blood is the patient so responsible for their own outcome. Expert patients, we're called, charged with the daily treatment of our terrible disease. And it's not constantly pricking yourself that rankles, nor the deep needle that seeds the cannula for an insulin pump, or getting the occasional swell of a black bruise when you nick a vein. Abstaining from sugar is a cinch if, like me, you've got a thing for salt – briny pickles, movie popcorn, fries hot from the fat bath. It's the fear that gets to you.

There are infinite fears. Among the worst, though, is the fear that you will fail at the dream of perfection, and they'll say something like, Well, she didn't take care of herself. Not enough. It wasn't enough.

Some days you feel like a violin played too long on the vibrato of a high note, string stressed to a snap. And people don't always cope the way you want them to. So when my mom says, He never took care of himself, I bluntly say, Don't blame him. She looks at me, tilts her head. She says, gently, You're nothing like him. I wish that made me feel better, too. But it wouldn't, even if it were true.

7.

Notes on Feelings of Failure

To honey the broken sauce
To comfort the truck-dragged dog until it's done
To hold very still while a doctor lasers away at your retina
To mourn alternate futures
To steer into the ice-slick skid
To find the email to a woman someone mentioned
To regret the cigarette from the night before
To say nothing, again
To envy a stranger for the smoothness of their hands
To hang up on someone you had thought a friend
To put off the blood-draw
To ignore the text
To still find yourself writing about this
To want to go back to a way things were
To watch your hair whiten and whiten
And other ways grief makes itself known in the mirror
To ask to be forgiven for your sorrow
To love someone who's gone
To ask to be forgiven for your body
To go on

8.

Short Essay On Those I Do Not Want to Fail

There's my mom, who sat on the edge of the bathtub patiently picking grit from my palm, wrist, elbow, after I sprawled myself from my bike, down the length of a gravel driveway. At the ER, they'd wanted to scrub it, but the pain blanked my brain like a TV shorted in a surge, and the Novocain they hoped would help kept oozing out of the wound. For hours, then, I soaked and sobbed, and she, calmly, bit by grain-of-sand-sized bit, picked me free.

There's my dad, who in my great seizure of need – a need to know, a need to unclench the fist that was my heart, a need to whisper the first goodbyes so there'd be room to take air in again – looked me in the eye, his moustache damp with tears, and answered my question – yes, baby, by now he's gone – and ransomed me.

There's the doctor who talked about Allen Ginsberg and Pink Martini while he looked at photographs of the backs of my eyes. There's the nurse-practitioner who told me she's never lost a patient to hypoglycemia unless it was on purpose, including her brother. There's the Italian doctor who, also diabetic, said – I, too, break the rules sometimes. How else could we survive?

There's Babette the Cat, small of foot and pink of nose, the magnitude of whose trust ever humbles me. And Waldo, pulled from a roofline. I contemplate his white fur so white it seems impossible that anything could be that bright and clean in this world for more than a single moment. Then he bites me.

And there's the life-raft full of friends forever netting me out of the seas. I once laughed atomized tomato soup all over one of them. He wiped his face with a smile. Another drank gin martinis with me for days while I sighed and sighed.

There's the beloved with a strawberry birthmark under his eye, who took me to Rome and changed all of my languages, and then one day he was suddenly petals blowing across a road I've never seen. And now there's the one whose bright blue compass rose tattoo over his heart is my way home.

And there's the children, mine if not my own, whose books on tape I have memorized and whose violet mascara I will borrow again and whose passenger-seat patter is the sound of a theory about futurity beginning to articulate itself, and who have needed me in ways that re-helixed my being.

And there's my sister, Emily. She said today, *I hate when either of us travels and we can't call, it's like I'm missing a limb.* Me too. The other day, she rang in a frenzy because one of her beloved chickens was covered in blood, blood all over the coop. She picked up the chicken, her black feathers flashing mermaid green in the afternoon sun, to find she'd only pulled off a toenail. *Jesus Christ,* said Em, *It looks like The goddamn Purge in here.* And when later, the yellow chicken named Dolly Parton died in her sleep, my sister didn't want to talk for a few days. When at last she answered the phone she said, amid weighty pauses, *If – you're going to have livestock – at some point – you're going to have – deadstock – but – right now – just – I just feel really sad – so – how are you?*

9.

Magic Words

This isn't going to be an overcoming story.

The doctor stands back from examining and

says, I know your retinas so well by now

I could pick them out of a line-up.

Later that day, he looks me in the eye

into which he's about to inject a small amount

of chemotherapy drugs, which should

slow the growth of blood vessels that will

otherwise only fissure and leak black smoke

into my vision and he says, you know

none of this is your fault. You just have

this terrible disease. And it feels

like being suddenly uncursed. When he

depresses the syringe into my open eye

I can see the potion flow in, like opening

my eyes underwater. Or like tearing up.

It eddies, then dissipates. I drive myself home.

10.

The Splendid Body

The splendid body is meat, flexor
and flesh pumping, pulling, anti-
gravity maverick just standing
upright all over museums and
in line for the bus and in the laundry
aisle where it's just standing there
smelling all the detergent like
it's no big deal. So what if a couple
of its squishy parts are suspended
within, like beach-bungled jellyfish
in a shelved jar, not doing anything?
Nothing on this side of the quantum
tunnel is perfect. The splendid body,
though, is splendid in the way
it keeps its steamy blood in, no matter
how bad it blushes. And splendid
in how it opens its mouth and
these invisible vibrations come
rippling out – if you put your wrist
right up to it when that happens
it feels somewhat like the feet
of many bees. The splendid body
loves the juniper smell of gin, loves
the warmth of printer-fresh paper,
and the sound fallen leaves make
under the wheel of a turning car.
If you touch it between the legs,
the splendid body will quicken
like bubbles in a just-on teakettle.
It knows it can't exist forever, so
it's collecting as many flavors as it can –
saffron, rainwater, fish-skin, chive.
Do not distract it from its purpose,
which is to feel everything it can find.

11.

To Gather Stones Together

Minneapolis. A few days after
my mother's January birthday.

My sister has also come to town.
We're paging through aisles of

white dresses so that my father,
whose cancer two months ago

turned his urine cochineal red
can walk me down the aisle next

Christmas. We talk about everything
but. They are asking me what kind

of dress do I want. I feel uninformed.
My sister holds a heavily sequined

garment away from herself, her
fingers grip it like scare quotes

and she winces, *So, like,* not *this.*
Champagne appears. I learn new

words: crepe, for a kind of textile,
sweep as a measure of length.

My father raises a beautiful gown
on its hanger. Sweetheart,

meaning how the neckline's cut.
Oh, I say, the only thing I know

is my pump has to hide right here,
my hand in the middle of my chest.

It's my mom who finds it, fine-boned
corset under supple ivory lengths

of heavy cloth. Off-the shoulder.
I try it on. I try it on with the pump.

I emerge, turn in it. My father rises.
The mirror holds us in its frame.

12.

Some Further Notes on the Impossible

Sort the grains. Gather the hank of golden wool. Fold a piece of paper in half twelve times. Make it new. Keep your blood sugars between 70 and 120. Brim the crystal vessel from the sacred stream. Make it to the bank Tuesday before they close. Reroute the rivers to the Augean Stables. Find an acre of land between the salt water and the strand. Improve upon the blank page. Carry well-water in this sieve. Weave that straw into gold. Smile more. You should smile. You should slay the many-headed hydra. Send the email. Wake the princess. Make it home before dark. Be capable of being in uncertainties, mysteries, doubts, without any irritable reaching after facts or reason. Slit the throat of the sacrificial lamb. Do not despair. Do not hope for a cure. Go to the underworld for a precious box. But here's the catch: For the task to count, you have to make it back.

Elegy for my Car, Wrecked on the Cape Highway

I'm so sorry, I wanted to comfort you
        sitting there in the Anchor Auto lot,

one headlight hanging loose, the other
        smashed in under the up-crumpled hood.

I wanted to say goodbye as if you were
        a lunged animal, a creature of hoof

or paw, who had a skull crushed in, not
        a radiator. And I felt responsible

because you were mine, because I was the one
        who made you spend your last good day

with the windshield wipers on, eight hours
        in the rain from Geneva, New York

to the end of the earth, where I was returning
        ten years later, and just forty minutes

from there, a fast highway exit, some traffic
        backed up, a chorus line of brake lights

rippling back to me too fast and I smashed
        your stop pedal to the floor, but it just

wasn't enough. And I hate it when things
        aren't enough, which seems to happen

quite a lot of the time. Here, perhaps,
        I'm more keen to the feeling, since

this is where I came to mourn my beloved
        who went missing, and for all I did, and

all his brother did, and for all the police
        did, and the Congresspeople and

Senators, not a trace of him was found. And I tried
        to rescue his daughter, and though

I can give her a roof, an allowance,
        someone to talk to, a kept promise,

I cannot give her what she needs, the
        childhood she never really had.

I buy her new jeans, she shows up
        in the same patched sweatpants, says

this is what anarchy looks like. Okay,
        I say, whatever frosts your cupcake,

and I really, really want to mean it,
        just as I really, really want to

mean it when I tell a student I don't
        take their angry email personally.

It's never enough, though I test my blood
        for sugar all day long, let the doctors

workshop my routines, consider my body,
        there is no cure for the disease I cannot

remember living without, nor the fears
        that are, for me, its worst complication.

And these things, and the trying-to-make-
        ends-meet which is also somehow

never quite enough (because one month
        there's a water leak driving up the bill,

the next my daughter pulls off the handle
        of you, the little silver car, because

the door was iced shut and she didn't
        realize). And there's the psychological

warfare of politicians whom I resist but
        letterhead stationary, early phone calls

might as well be burnt as offerings
        in my bathtub, pleas ashing in my mouth.

I was driving you far from the bills
        and the clamor of everybody's panic

so I could return to this place where I can
        listen to the sand blown up on the street

grind beneath my feet as I stride the ocean-
        side blocks of town, or the waves

shushing up into the breakwater. It's bleak
        here, austere in my favorite ways,

and calms me. When I drove out here ten years
        ago, grieving, guilt-winnowed, nerves

shrill with a singular purpose – it was to finish
        a conversation that had ended

before it was over for me, to write the rest
        of my own side, to say goodbye,

and maybe that's why I've been having
        such confusing dreams. The smells

of salt-brined cedarwood and new lilac
        remind me in ways I am not fully aware

that there's some symmetry here, in this
        fearful motion from then to now.

My future husband tells me I am not a bad
        person for having had a car wreck

and my sister tells me I am not a bad person
        for having a future husband now,

and I know they're both telling me the truth.
        But another truth is this: I am not good

at saying goodbye. So I cry, and I founder,
        and the nice man at Anchor Auto says,

It's okay. We develop relationships with cars.
        And I'm reminded of an old IKEA ad,

anthropomorphizing a lamp left stooped
        in a rainy gutter while the new one glows

in a cozy window and then a man with a German
        accent says, *The lamp has no feelings –*

And for a moment I feel humor as relief. Still,
        this car brought me into my own future

many times. You brought me here, and back
      and forth to the retinal specialist in Utah

and out of Utah, when a whiskey-ed up man
      said to me the cruelest things I'd ever heard.

You brought me to a new job at a steepled
      brick university, despite the snows –

Thank you, for being my independence
      at times when I needed it most. Thanks

for helping me to get away, when away
      is where I needed to be. And thank you

for, in the end, bringing me home safely,
      for taking that final blow, so I did not.

Within

1.

Inside of every curse
is its own cure –

the handsome prince
frogged or beasted,

perhaps revealing
something of his nature

must be loved
(to lift the spell)

despite his less-than
human looks, body

more like pet, or predator.
But the joke's on

whoever cast the bones,
for the love that solves

(nevermind the kink)
is deeper and more loyal

than he'd even think
or hope for, untransformed.

2.

Every great debut
has a duet at its core –

Nobody ever wrote
an opera alone, nor

a novel, somewhere
in the mix, someone

else made soup, took
the kids to the dentist,

listened intently and
quibbled with the way

the villain is portrayed.
Every sculpture has

its model, every poem
its muse, or at least

somewhere buried in it,
its 'him' or 'her' or 'yous'.

3.

Within any romance
is a coma we've all

been in – the drowse
of heavy-lidded love

that makes us believe
our beloveds. Asleep

in our towers, thorned in,
spindle-pricked, we loll

and drool in wonder
at this swoon we feel.

But it's not true love
that wakes us with a kiss –

remember this – it is
betrayal's icy hand

beneath the quilt, his
soft hiss, his look of guilt.

6.

Most wisdom is come by
a long, hard swim

from the dim sea floor
of feeling (what is it?)

to the surface. Sensing
closeness, the self emerges

gasping. Like waters
spangled with light,

the right words brighten
the mind and give relief –

whether from sorrow,
grief, or just confusion –

and they'll keep, those
words. You'll need them

for the next time (and
there will be one, of course)

you feel, or fail. Or fall
in love, or under a curse.

Productions of Failure

Everywhere I look I find

a hole. After a sentence,

what's unsaid. Between us,

space unclosed by embrace.

On pages I lately write,

hard return after hard return

to thoughts I seem only to have

by fragment. There is a ghost-

hole in the laundry closet wall.

I worry the cat will go in so

the door is always shut. There's

a hole in the future tense,

more *we shoulds* than *wills*,

conjugations of wish riddling

our promises. There's a hole

in my husband that he hasn't yet

lowered his dead brother into.

I observe this cratered landscape

like an astronaut planting a flag

where nobody's flag belongs.

Table of Contents: An Aspirational

inspired by Renee Gladman

Poem that rises like seeded bread
Poem that softens the knots of the heavy-worked
Poem commemorating a protest after which the monuments were draped
permanently in black silk
Poem that is actually a recipe for a lemon curd I can eat
Poem that is actually a spell for returning sea water to the slow-creaking ice
where it belonged
Poem for the defenestration of tyrants
Poem that, read aloud, sounds like a cello played on a crystal floor
Erasure poem, slowly removing each cruel comment from existence
Poem written without words about things known and felt beyond words, felt
and known deep in the star-forming nebulae of the body known as the pillars of
creation
Poem nobody needs
Poem everybody needs, and which completes those needs
Poem that swells like a pink balloon when read, swells, swells, and then bursts
Poem that vigils, that tends the flame, poem that enwonders
Poem spent as a lung from singing out
Poem blithe as a witch unhunted
Poem faintly bouqueted with rosewater and bergamot when you open its page
Poem reminding boneheads we aren't NPCs in their tournament of buffoonery
Poem to sigh a stillborn awake
Poem consecrating the time a woman who never had before, came
Poem to summon the angels of science, that will shrink a tumor if read
Poem pealing through the dark like an ancient bell
Poem that sleeks, that satins, ravenous poem
Poem that is a riot of wings
Unctuous poem, that renders into velvety sauce in the mouth
Poem that bricks the walls back together once the floods recede
Poem spooked as a skinny dog
Poem prim and proper as statuary
Poem acknowledging that we may not overcome this, but that one day the
world will end and everything will be fine

Poem that coaxes the hatchling from its speckled egg
Poem to soothe the tiny keening of a mouse widowed by a murderous cat
Poem that tastes like rosemary ice cream, or champagne
Poem perfect for a perfect day
Poem for those who do not read or write poems, too
Poem that is a map of the world the size of the world
and lessens the ache of all who add to it

Introduction to a Poem at a Reading

I wrote this poem on a very cold day in Cincinnati. It is partly in response to having just taught Pablo Neruda, from whence the epigraph "Es tan corto el amor, y es tan largo el olvido." "It's so short, love is, and forgetting so long." (Oh, Neruda. I still feel so betrayed.) What else do you need to know? I guess you could say I'm good with the dead. I find they're shy but loyal, and ask only that we leave out oranges occasionally, and now and then speak their names quietly when nobody else is around. You might also want to know that when I was on my way home from talking about Neruda, a man on the radio was talking about the human heart – how all the blood in the human body passes through it once per minute, how it works so hard a human heart could drain a swimming pool in less than a week, and how (to do the very first open-heart surgery, on a child) doctors sewed the boy's circulatory system into his father's, so his father's heart pumped the child's blood along with his own through both of their bodies, while doctors paused the boy's heart and emptied it of blood and sewed closed a hole in one of its lobes. And I think of my father who has driven me across the arteries of this nation many times, many emergency times. And then, of how the surgery worked, but the boy died of pneumonia several days later anyway. And then the father's heart, which only days before had been moving his son's blood around in his own body, "broke," we say. As if the heart were brittle, which it rarely is, though it is always, always fragile. When I took my Yaya to her congestive heart failure doctor, he said that a healthy heart is like a balloon. When you take a flight of stairs two at a time, or have rowdy kitchen-table sex, or when you suddenly get terrifying news over the phone that you absolutely were not expecting, your heart expands, swells with more blood, then later relaxes back to size. Congestive heart failure stiffens the muscle, so it can't. Then, the doctor said, it's more like a teacup. And the lungs fill with fluid, and fluid pools in the wrists and ankles. To give a little context, my Yaya would have let them sew her onto her son, would have used her own heart to pump his blood, too, even after she got sick, but that would not have saved him. She would talk about him sometimes. She became angry when she told me how the doctors wouldn't believe her when she insisted he was deaf. She got sad when she talked about his marriages, first to a waitress with a real mean streak, and then to a postal worker with a TV shopping addiction. To give a little context, he had the same disease I do, and it killed him. First it took his eyes, then his kidneys, then his hands and feet, and it turns out you can survive awhile without those things, but not without a heart. So I did some research and, it turns out, ancient Greeks believed the heart was where the human soul dwelled, and a city named Cyrene was probably responsible for the heart-shaped icon that in no way resembles an anatomical organ. Their cash crop was silphium, a contraceptive plant, whose seed pod gave Cyrene the shape of its coins and us our symbol for love. I texted it to my daughter the other day, that symbol. Light purple. She texted one back but colored black. For sorrow. To give a little context, her heart is fine but her brain works differently than other people's. Faster, like mine or yours if we were in a kind of panic, and it won't slow down and give her any peace. I cannot help her, which makes my heart sag heavy. To give a little context, I inherited her. My daughter. From a man I loved very much. But love is short, while forgetting is long. So very long. Letting aside *can* you forget, do you have to? Because I felt my heart expand the other day when I watched a man I love now fill a water balloon for his son, so his son could throw it at us. Which he did, but missed us and hit the dirt near us and got dirt all over us and laughed. And that made us, all dirt-covered, laugh. And to give a little context, I told that man I love he should write a poem with the word *heart* in the title, which he did, and that man told me I should end my poems on images more often, and he was very convincing, which is why this poem ends as it does, on the image of a wooden anatomical model of the human heart in flames.

He Asks Me to Send Him Some Words (Here in His Garden)

Hammock. Red. It held us we held on I used my legs and later you knelt down. Hand. Inner knee. Shoulder tattoo. Tattoo where your heart stampedes. Later. Red glass wine glass. Sun. Red chair rocking forward. Cracked stone slabs. Stone table. Sunned stone. Sun on my naked feet. Ginko. Bamboo. Sandbox. Begonia growing out of an old chimenea. Bird bath. Sweetgum. Fronds. Nearly empty, the good bourbon. Stock pot. At last night's crawfish boil she said. It was funny. Red wagon. Bird red as that wagon, on it. Lipstick on the rim of a plastic cup. Fig tree. Busted trampoline. This red splendor. Dappled. This green shade. This place we come to by our patience. I breathe your fire. This hope. So hard it feels as sure as all the red.

Acknowledgments

The following poems have appeared in the following publications, sometimes in earlier forms:

Academy of American Poets: "The Splendid Body";
American Poetry Review: "At Teufelsberg in the Subjunctive Mood";
Best American Poetry 2019/Southern Indiana Review: "A Brief History of the Future Apocalypse";
Copper Nickel: "Chronic Illness Imagined as a Haunting";
The Journal: "Elegy for My Car, Wrecked on the Cape Highway";
The Missouri Review: "To My Insulin Pump," "Spiel: A Love Poem," "The Woodpecker," "Discourses of Diabetes Care," "Ohio";
Prelude: "Studies from Childhood";
Seneca Review: "The Beelitz Heilstätten";
Tin House: "Ode to Anthony Bourdain";
Tupelo Quarterly: "Sligo Abbey," "He Asks Me to Send Him Some Words (Here in My House)," "I Ask Him to Send Me Some Words (Reading the Florida Handbook)," "He Asks Me to Send Him Some Words (Here in His Garden)."

This work has been supported by an Amy Lowell Scholarship for American Poets Traveling Abroad, an Ohio Arts Council Individual Excellence Award, and a Summer Research Fellowship from the Taft Humanities Center at the University of Cincinnati. Without the generous moral and material support provided by these awards, the vast majority of this book could never have come to be.

First and foremost, this book is for my family. Thank you to my parents, Nancy and Steve Lindenberg, for their unwavering support, even when I write about them, even when I remember things wrong, even when it isn't the whole story – the truth is that their unconditional love helps make poems possible that might otherwise be very scary to write. I'm deeply and enduringly grateful to them for raising me to be an insatiable reader, and for the accursed work ethic I inherited from them, and for their relentless advocacy. Thank you, too, for taking me to the Barbara Davis Diabetes Center all those years of my childhood and youth, and all the other sacrifices I know you made to help me live as easily as possible with the impossible. I am also enduringly, profoundly, and affectionately thankful to my sister, Emily Zuccaro, who also made sacrifices, and who lets me quote her all the time, because she is wittier than I am, and less afraid than I am to call things out – including sometimes me. And thank you to my three beautiful children, Robin and Lila and Ethan, for loving me and accepting me and letting me love you all (and write about you all) as my own.

This project began many years ago. I found myself in Berlin thanks to the Amy Lowell award, surrounded by different forms of ruin and repair resulting from multiple wars and the city's in-some-ways-ongoing reunification. I found myself fixating on the idea of these ruins. Foremost, they operate for me as a kind of archive, an unwritten and untranslatable record of events that changed their location and environment again and again. I became very aware that no such space is 'innocent,' and there is a real risk that ruins might give us the impression that we are somehow in the future of these architectures and spaces and the things they represent (like: religious oppression, U.S. American imperialism, genocidal antisemitism, tyrannical industrialization). But that's not to say that nothing ever changes – hence in these poems, a ruined Abbey becomes the site of multigenerational matrilineal connection and magic, a decrepit spy station for listening in on enemies becomes a space for romance and contradiction and an extended meditation on "what-ifs," while a destroyed factory becomes a space of repose and reflection, and so forth. Rather than finding myself drawn to the decay of these spaces, I found myself drawn more to their persistence and their transformation. I owe an debt of gratitude to Hoschi Lewerenz, who was often my guide, sometimes my partner in breaking-and-entering, occasionally my bodyguard, and always my patient, kind, and generous companion as he led me to many of the places that appear in these pages (and many others that do not) while I tried to understand why what it was about ruins that so compelled me.

The project took a rather unexpected turn when the Covid-19 pandemic erupted into the world in spring of 2020. I found myself less interested in writing about ruin and decay as ruin and decay felt closer and closer to home. I began to see the words "diabetic" and "severe outcome" or "death" within centimeters of each other in newspapers, online articles, medical journals, and CDC guidelines. The fear, the sense of imminent and mortal threat, was inescapable. Since I could not bring myself to think about anything else, I allowed myself to indulge in writing about this very scary disease with which I have lived for the last thirty-five years, and with which I will almost certainly live the rest of my life. Some of my interest in ruin clarified itself for me as I became more conscious of how hard I work to maintain a functional human body, how quickly and irreversibly it could decay, and how elusive the possibility of restoration. I came to articulate my frustration with the goal of perfection and value the simple intentional keeping-on, with the hopes of deferring the inevitable as long as possible. And I realized how much the dread and anxiety (and denial) I have often felt myself looked and felt to me like the dread and anxiety (and denial) I saw in people across the world dealing with the sudden ubiquity of a life-threatening disease (from which the world as an organism will likely never be cured). The more I wrote, the more everything felt connected, related, impacted by the fact of human mortality and the various ways we individually and collectively confront and interact with and respond to it. And I could not have done the work, either the work on the page or the hours and days and weeks of work that preceded the page, without my husband and literary partner Chris Hayes, whose generosity I would describe as "unimaginable," except that every bit of it has been real, felt, true, and invaluable. He kept me safe and he kept me sane throughout the writing of this project. There is no way to express my comprehensive gratitude. I love you. Thank you, thank you, thank you.

I have a small hagiography of friends and literary colleagues without whom this book would not exist, and certainly would not be any good. They gave so generously of their time, their keen and rigorous attention, their openness and honesty and support as I was writing, or thinking about, or sending out these poems and/or this manuscript. For reading, talking, supporting, editing, commenting, and keeping me honest, I want to thank Ada Limón, Donald Revell, Felicia Zamora, John Drury, Kathryn Cowles, Geoff Babbitt, Timothy O'Keefe, Erin Belieu, Jessica Piazza, Jill Alexander Essbaum, and Sara Eliza Johnson, and I'm certain there are people I'm failing to mention here who deserve and have my gratitude, as well.

Thank you to the incredible team at BOA Editions for believing in this book and bringing it into being. I am grateful and extremely proud to be part of this press and its community.

And thank you, you who have read these words.

About the Author

Rebecca Lindenberg is the author of *Love, an Index* (McSweeney's, 2012) and *The Logan Notebooks* (Mountain West Poetry Series, 2014), winner of the 2015 Utah Book Award. She's the recipient of an Amy Lowell Scholarship for American Poets Traveling Abroad, a National Endowment for the Arts Grant in Literature, an Ohio Arts Council Individual Excellence Award, a Dorothy Sargent Rosenberg Prize, and residency fellowship at the Fine Arts Work Center in Provincetown and the MacDowell Arts Colony. She's an Associate Professor of Poetry at the University of Cincinnati, where she also serves as Poetry Editor for the *Cincinnati Review*.

BOA Editions, Ltd. American Poets Continuum Series

120

Colophon

BOA Editions, Ltd., a not-for-profit publisher of poetry
and other literary works, fosters readership and appreciation
of contemporary literature. By identifying, cultivating, and publishing both
new and established poets and selecting authors of unique literary talent,
BOA brings high-quality literature to the public.

Support for this effort comes from the sale of its publications,
grant funding, and private donations.

*

*The publication of this book is made possible, in part,
by the special support of the following individuals:*

Anonymous

Angela Bonazinga & Catherine Lewis

Mr. & Mrs. P. David Caccamise, *in memory of Dr. Gary H. Conners*

Bernadette Catalana

Daniel R. Cawley

Bonnie Garner

Margaret B. Heminway

Charles Hertrick & Joan Gerrity

Grant Holcomb, *in memory of Robert & Willy Hursh*

Kathleen C. Holcombe

Nora A. Jones

Paul LaFerriere & Dorrie Parini, *in honor of Bill Waddell*

Jack & Gail Langerak

Barbara Lovenheim

Joe McElveney

Boo Poulin

David W. Ryon

John H. Schultz

William Waddell & Linda Rubel